SCIENTISTS AND THEIR DISCOVERIES

ALBERT EINSTEIN

SCIENTISTS AND THEIR DISCOVERIES

SCIENTISTS AND THEIR DISCOVERIES

ALBERT EINSTEIN

DERRICK RAIN

MASON CREST

Mason Crest
450 Parkway Drive, Suite D
Broomall, Pennsylvania 19008
(866) MCP-BOOK (toll-free)
www.masoncrest.com

CPSIA Compliance Information: Batch #SG2018.
For further information, contact Mason Crest at 1-866-MCP-Book.

First printing
9 8 7 6 5 4 3 2 1

Library of Congress Cataloging-in-Publication Data

ISBN: 978-1-4222-4024-3 (hc)
ISBN: 978-1-4222-7756-0 (ebook)

Scientists and their Discoveries series ISBN: 978-1-4222-4023-6

Developed and Produced by National Highlights Inc.
Interior and cover design: Yolanda Van Cooten
Production: Michelle Luke

CONTENTS

KEY ICONS TO LOOK FOR:

Words to understand: These words with their easy-to-understand definitions will increase the reader's understanding of the text while building vocabulary skills.

Sidebars: This boxed material within the main text allows readers to build knowledge, gain insights, explore possibilities, and broaden their perspectives by weaving together additional information to provide realistic and holistic perspectives.

Educational videos: Readers can view videos by scanning our QR codes, providing them with additional educational content to supplement the text. Examples include news coverage, moments in history, speeches, iconic sports moments, and much more!

Text-dependent questions: These questions send the reader back to the text for more careful attention to the evidence presented there.

Research projects: Readers are pointed toward areas of further inquiry connected to each chapter. Suggestions are provided for projects that encourage deeper research and analysis.

Series glossary of key terms: This back-of-the-book glossary contains terminology used throughout the series. Words found here increase the reader's ability to read and comprehend higher-level books and articles in this field.

During the first half of the twentieth century, the discoveries of physicist Albert Einstein changed the way that humans understood the universe and how it works.

WORDS TO UNDERSTAND

first–class degree: the highest classification of a European university degree, indicating high academic achievement.

Maxwell's theory of electricity and magnetism: Laws governing electrical and magnetic forces and the behavior of light (and radio) waves.

Patents Office: a government department issuing copyright on inventions.

polytechnic: an institution of higher education offering courses in many subjects, especially vocational or technical subjects.

scientific paper: an article reporting original scientific work.

CHAPTER 1

Early Life

In ancient Greece some 3,000 years ago, men began asking questions about the fundamental nature of the world, and all the activities within it. In this way they began the study of physics. The problem of physics was to find a simple explanation for the way nature worked. Thus they observed water, and noticed that when it was heated, it always changed into vapor. They observed the regular sequence of night and day, and of the seasons. They recognized that as the world changes, it changes in a regular way, and they tried to develop scientific laws that explained how nature works.

For more than 2,000 years, the scientific theories of Aristotle and other Greek philosophers were considered by Western scholars to provide an accurate understanding of how the world truly works. But in the sixteenth century, some European scientists began to question these ancient teachings. Their answers did not always please an all-powerful Christian Church, one of the dominant institutions of European life at this time. For daring to suggest that the earth rotates, Giordano Bruno (1548–1600) was burned at the stake. Galileo Galilei (1564–1642) made a similar assertion, and was imprisoned and forced to confess his error. Nevertheless, the earth does rotate. The Church could hinder scientific progress, but could not stop it.

The seventeenth century saw the development of scientific instruments, such as the telescope, which enabled men to make more detailed observations and discover new facts. There were also major advances in the European knowledge of mathematics, which allowed simple relations between the new facts to be stated clearly in mathematical formulas. The greatest figure of the period was English scientist Sir Isaac Newton (1642–1727). Newton established laws that explained

English mathematician Sir Isaac Newton (1642–1727) is one of the greatest figures in the history of science. His Law of Universal Gravitation and his theories of motion were among the most important scientific discoveries of the seventeenth century.

how things moved. Using his laws of motion, he could solve a range of problems, from the time it takes for a falling apple to hit the ground to the motion of the moon.

Newton's laws were highly accurate in almost all cases. However, in the nineteenth century, new discoveries were made that could not be fully explained by Newton's laws. Ludwig Boltzmann (1844–1906) developed a new theory of heat that made it possible to calculate how a gas would behave when heated. This could be used to make steam engines more efficient. The laws of electricity and the properties of magnets were discovered by James Clerk Maxwell (1831–79), leading to the development of electric motors. These laws enabled physicists to better understand what light is. Again, as the nineteenth century drew to a close, there was a feeling among scientists that man really understood how nature works.

But again, this was not so. As new experiments were carried out, new results were found that did not work with the existing theories. At first, some scientists thought that minor changes to the mathematical formulas would resolve the problems. As the failures of the old theories increased, however, it became clear that this was not so. What was needed was a change in the way people thought about the problems. The new theories would be very different from the ideas of the previous four centuries. Many scientists would contribute to a changing understanding of how the world works in the first three decades of the twentieth century. None of them contributed more of lasting value than Albert Einstein.

Einstein's Early Life

Albert Einstein was born on March 14, 1879, in Ulm, a small town in southern Germany. Albert's mother, Pauline, to whom he was always deeply attached, came from a family of moderate wealth. Two years before he was born, they had helped Hermann Einstein, Albert's father, to set up a small engineering workshop. They helped again when the business failed a year after Albert's birth, and the family moved to nearby Munich. Hermann Einstein was a jovial, well-meaning man, but he was not serious enough to make a success of his business. However, with the aid of his wife's relations, he was able to provide a comfortable home for his wife, his son, and his daughter Maja, born two years after Albert.

Albert's parents were Jews, but they were, it seems, not very strict in the faith. When the time came for Albert to go to school, when he was five years old, he was sent to the Catholic school, simply because it was near the family's home.

At the same age, Albert began to learn to play the violin under his mother's guidance. The violin always remained important to him, and in later life he became quite a good amateur player.

Scan here for a short video tour of the historic city of Ulm, Germany:

Albert was a quiet child. He had a normal childhood and there was little to characterize him as a future genius. In fact, he was late in learning to walk, and did not speak fluently until he was nine. At first he was even thought of as a somewhat backward child. All this had changed completely by the time he reached his teens.

At the age of seven, Einstein started to learn algebra with his uncle Jacob, and by the age of thirteen he had mastered a good deal of mathematics. He had also started to study physics and philosophy under the guidance of Max Talmey, a friend some years older than himself. Talmey recommended that Albert should read the works of the great German philosopher Immanuel Kant (1724–1804). Later, Talmey wrote, "At that time he was still a child, only thirteen years old, yet Kant's works, incomprehensible to ordinary mortals, seemed to be clear to him."

Yet to Albert's teachers at school, this did not seem to be so. At the age of ten he

Albert Einstein and his sister, Maja, at home in Ulm, c. 1886.

The Danube River flows through the medieval city of Ulm, where Albert Einstein was born in 1879.

had started at the local secondary school, the Luitpold Gymnasium, where he was very unhappy. He rebelled against the rigid discipline, and was horrified at the fear used in the teaching methods there. The teachers considered him an unruly child. In 1894, after another business failure, his father moved to Italy. The school was not sorry to lose an unpromising pupil who, in the words of a teacher, "could not be expected to make a success of anything." Albert was not sorry to leave. He took with him a hatred of pointless rules and regulations and a distrust of authority. Only one year after leaving the Luitpold Gymnasium, he insisted on giving up his German nationality. This was an unusual step for a boy of fifteen, although not as difficult as it would be today.

Scottish physicist James Clerk Maxwell (1831–79) unified the laws of electricity and magnetism, thereby discovering the nature of light and radio waves. Maxwell was also known for his work on the behavior of gases.

A monument to German philosopher Immanuel Kant, whose writings had a great influence on young Einstein. Kant's major work was his Critique of Pure Reason, published in 1781. It explained his philosophy that knowledge results from both experience and pure thought.

Einstein's next move was to Zurich, to sit for the entrance examinations for the **polytechnic** there. His first attempt was a failure. He distinguished himself only in mathematics, for he had done little to prepare for the exam. After a year's schooling in Zurich, he was allowed to take the exam again. This time, he passed.

Beginning His Work

Young Einstein was now beginning to think about physics, and in particular about electricity and magnetism. His first experience with magnetic effects had come at the age of five, in a famous incident. His father had shown him a pocket compass, and Albert had observed how the compass needle always pointed in one direction, toward the north. He is reported to have grasped immediately the very difficult idea of a force transmitted through empty space. This force acts on the compass needle to keep it pointing in that one direction. Now, at the age of sixteen, Einstein wrote a short essay on the subject of magnetic forces. He sent it to his uncle Cäsar Koch, with whom he maintained a close relationship for many years.

Einstein worked very hard while attending the Polytechnic Institute in Zurich, but not at the lectures and courses he was supposed to attend. These were too boring and old-fashioned for him. With increasing arrogance and self-confidence, he worked at what he considered important. He spent much of his time studying **theories of electricity and magnetism** that had been proposed some years earlier by the great Scottish physicist, James Clerk Maxwell. "In view of the standards of university teaching," Einstein was later to comment, "it is surprising that knowledge did not long ago die out."

Nevertheless, when the time came for him to take his degree examinations at the end of his fourth year at the polytechnic, he passed with the highest honors. He achieved this with the help of his friend Marcel Grossmann, whose lecture notes he borrowed and studied for the exams.

In 1900 a bright young man with a **first–class degree** might expect to find a position to stay at a university to carry out some research on his own ideas. Such positions were found for Einstein's colleagues, but for arrogant young Einstein, who "would not be told anything," his professors at the polytechnic found they had no room.

TQUAI.

This colored postcard shows Zurich, Switzerland, c. 1900. The large building with the square roof is the Polytechnic Institute, which Einstein attended from 1896 to 1900.

For the next two years, Einstein was forced to accept various temporary teaching and research jobs between periods of unemployment. He was, however, far from idle. His first **scientific paper**—an article containing his original work—was published in a scientific journal in 1900, the year he left the polytechnic. This formed the basis of a thesis for the degree of Doctor of Philosophy the following year. But with no job, and no prospects, Einstein seemed to the world to be a failure.

It was Grossmann who eventually came to the rescue once again. He persuaded his father to use his influence with some friendly Government officials, and a position was found for Einstein in the **Patents Office** in Berne.

So, at the age of twenty-three, Albert Einstein became a Swiss Civil Servant (third class).

 TEXT-DEPENDENT QUESTIONS

1. What did Scottish physicist James Clerk Maxwell study and create laws that reflected the behavior of?
2. In what town was Albert Einstein born?
3. In what European city did Einstein study at the polytechnic?

 RESEARCH PROJECT

Albert Einstein once described the work of Scottish physicist James Clerk Maxwell as the "most profound and the most fruitful that physics has experienced since the time of Newton." Using your school library or the internet, find out more about the life of James Clerk Maxwell. How did his discoveries influence and inspire Einstein? Write a two-page report and share it with your class.

The Museum of Albert Einstein in Berne, Switzerland. Einstein and his wife rented an apartment on the second floor of this building at Kramgasse No. 49 from 1903 to 1905.

WORDS TO UNDERSTAND

atom: the smallest unit of matter that can be obtained by chemical means.

laws of dynamics: laws which govern the motion of objects subject to forces.

spacetime diagram: a two-dimensional graph that depicts events as happening in a universe consisting of one space dimension (on the horizontal axis) and one time dimension (on the vertical axis). Mathematician Hermann Minkowski, a former teacher of Einstein's in Zurich, developed the current form of this diagram in 1908.

uniform motion: motion in a straight line at a never changing speed.

CHAPTER 2

Man from the Ministry

For the next seven years, Albert Einstein was known to most of those who knew him at all as a man who had started on an undistinguished career in the Civil Service. He had taken up Swiss nationality. He liked living in Berne. He enjoyed his work. No one could guess the dramatic changes that were about to take place.

In 1903, after a year at the Patents Office, Einstein married Mileva Marie, the daughter of a Slav peasant family. She had been in the same class as Einstein at the Zurich Polytechnic, and was the only student in that physics class to fail the final examination.

Einstein's reasons for marriage were not at all clear. Perhaps he thought of a wife as someone to run a house for him. Mileva was not entirely suited to that task. If Einstein had thought that marriage would leave him with more free time, he was to be disappointed. Perhaps he drifted almost absent-mindedly into marriage. Perhaps, as he later said to a friend, he married Mileva only because she had "such a lovely voice."

The couple had two sons, Hans Albert, born in 1904 and Eduard, born six years later. We get a sad impression of the family's home life in Berne from a colleague visiting them several years after the marriage:

> The door of the apartment was open to allow the floor which had just been scrubbed, as well as the washing hung up in the hall, to dry. I entered Einstein's room. With one hand he was calmly rocking a cradle. In his mouth he had a very bad cigar, and in the other hand an open book. The stove was smoking horribly. How in the world could he bear it?

Austrian physicist Ludwig Boltzmann (1844–1906) was a pioneer of the theory that atoms are real, and can be seen in motion.

THE MICHELSON-MORLEY EXPERIMENT

In 1887 two American scientists, Albert Michelson and Edward Morley, carried out a famous experiment to demonstrate the existence of a substance called "aether." People thought that light needed aether to travel through space, just as sound waves needed air to travel. They thought the Earth made an "aether wind" as it traveled around the Sun, and that the speed at which a beam of light traveled could vary according to whether it was going with or against the aether wind.

Michelson and Morley discovered that it didn't matter how you measured the speed of light, the answer was always the same. The light always traveled at about 186,000 miles per second (300,000 km per second). The speed didn't change, even if the source of the light beam or the person doing the measuring was moving. This result was later confirmed by many other experiments. It seemed that there was no aether after all.

Scientists tried to come up with explanations, including some that sounded very bizarre, for this result. Some suggested that the Earth dragged the aether around with it so there was no wind. Others thought that objects shrank as they moved through the aether. Or the reason that the speed of light seemed to be the same in all directions was that the equipment the scientists used to measure the speed had changed size. It was up to Einstein to propose a better way to explain that the speed of light in a vacuum is constant.

Einstein was always able to bear it. He could shut out distractions from his mind, with the result that he could work anywhere.

Working With Friends

Soon after his arrival in Berne, he had advertised in the local newspaper to give private lessons in physics. He quickly attracted a first pupil, Maurice Solovine, and then a second, Konrad Habicht, and the three became close friends. They called themselves the Olympian Academy. The lessons soon changed to discussions of scientific and philosophical problems. The group would meet in cafés, or in Einstein's home, or sometimes walk with him on his way home from work. Cut off from the academic world, this was Einstein's only opportunity to talk about physics. And it was physics that was his only real interest.

In 1904 he helped Michelangelo Besso, an Italian engineer, to find a position in the Patents Office. Besso and Einstein became firm friends, and it is from their correspondence that we know much about Einstein's life. It was with Besso that he now discussed the new ideas that were beginning to take shape in his mind.

By 1905 he was ready to announce these ideas to the world. They were published in four major scientific papers in the *Annals of Physics,* an important scientific journal in Germany. Any one of these articles would have brought him recognition by his fellow physicists. These four articles contributed a great deal to the foundation of modern physics and changed the existing ideas about space, time, mass, and energy. The second article, on the kinetic theory of gases, was an important contribution to establishing the reality of **atoms**.

In the early twentieth century, many—but not all—scientists believed that matter was composed of tiny particles in a set pattern that were in constant motion. The particles were called "atoms" and this idea was called the "atomic hypothesis." Chemical reactions could be explained in terms of atoms. Austrian physicist Ludwig Boltzmann (1844–1906) had developed a theory that could explain the behavior of gases, assuming them to consist of atoms. The question remained: Was Boltzmann's theory just a convenient way to describe what was happening, or did atoms really exist? Boltzmann had been driven insane by attacks on his opinion that atoms were real. Even at the beginning of this century, the question had still not been settled.

Scottish botanist Robert Brown (1773–1858) observed the motion of particles suspended in liquid; their seemingly random movements became known as Brownian motion. Einstein's 1905 paper used Brownian motion as support for the existence of atoms, explaining that the crazy motion of the particle is caused by atoms in the liquid striking it from all directions.

It could only be settled finally if one could actually see an atom, or at least the effect of its motion. There was one important piece of experimental evidence. In 1828 Scottish botanist Robert Brown (1773–1858) had observed through a microscope the motion of pollen grains suspended in a liquid. The motion was later named after him, as "Brownian motion." Einstein now explained this motion as due to the effect of the atoms of the liquid striking the pollen grains. He worked out the motion one would expect on the basis of the atomic hypothesis. This was found to agree with the observed motion. Scientists had come as close as possible at the time to seeing an individual atom. The resistance to accepting atoms as real collapsed.

For a short lesson on spacetime diagrams, scan here:

The Marriage of Space and Time

The third of Einstein's articles of 1905 contained a theory about space and time that would mark a turning point in physics. It was the theory of relativity. Einstein later said, "Between the conception of the idea of this Special Theory of Relativity and the completion of the corresponding publication, there elapsed five or six weeks. But the arguments and building blocks were being prepared over a period of years." After many fruitless attempts and periods of confusion, Einstein said, "at last it came to me that time itself was suspect."

Portrait of Einstein at the Berne Patents Office, taken around the time he was composing the papers that would make him internationally famous. Scientists often refer to the year 1905 as the annus mirabilis —Einstein's year of miracles.

On June 5, 1905—a few weeks before Einstein's first paper on relativity—French mathematician Henri Poincaré (1854–1912) published a paper that came very close to touching on Einstein's theory. "It seems that this impossibility of demonstrating absolute motion is a general law of nature," Poincaré wrote. In their writings the two scientists never acknowledged each others' work.

To understand what Einstein mean when he said that "time itself was suspect," we need to understand one simple idea. Imagine two trains side by side on parallel tracks. The carriages of each train are numbered from one to four. In each carriage there is an accurate clock. Suppose that one of the trains is stationary and the other is moving slowly past it. The guard in the rear carriage of the moving train notes the time at which he passes each of the carriages of the stationary train. At seven o'clock exactly he passes carriage number one, five seconds later he passes the second carriage, five seconds after that he passes the third, and so on.

Now suppose a person is sitting in the last carriage of the stationary train, and it is nighttime. The guard will see the lights of the moving train slowly passing him. He will find it difficult to tell which of the two trains is moving. But he will have a different perspective than the passenger in the stationary train, or a passenger in the moving train. And an astronaut, if he were to watch all this from space, would say that all of them are wrong. From his perspective the astronaut could see that while one train is stationary on the earth, the earth itself is moving, so that neither of the trains is actually in the same place at the various times!

To ancient Greek scientists, it was obvious that it must be possible to say what is meant by "the same place at different times." In their view, then, it must be possible to draw the true **spacetime diagram** in just one way, with the vertical lines representing the same places at different times, and the sloping lines representing objects in motion. It took 2,000 years and the genius of Galileo and Newton to realize that this was not so. Their **laws of dynamics**—the theory of how objects move—showed that no experiment with material objects will enable us to say who is really at rest and who is moving with **uniform motion**; that is, in one direction at a constant speed. Only the motion of one system *relative* to another is detectable. However, Newton's laws apply only to the motion of all *material* objects. They cannot be used to describe the behavior of light. For this we need the electromagnetic theory discovered by James Clerk Maxwell. If we cannot do an experiment with material objects to discover our motion, perhaps we can do one with light.

Let us go back to the train example of the two trains, and put a light source at one end of a carriage of each train and a mirror at the other. According to the laws of Newton and Maxwell, a flash of light should take a certain time to travel from one end of the carriage to the mirror and back again. Calculations derived from Newton's and Maxwell's theories of light and motion indicate that the length of time should be greater in the moving train than in the stationary one. According to the existing theories, light should travel more slowly in the moving train because it takes longer to go from one end of the carriage and back again.

Imagine the bewilderment that followed the result of such an experiment in 1887 when it was found that the two lengths of time were exactly the same! Either Maxwell's theory of light or Newton's laws of mechanics must be wrong.

Einstein had foreseen the problem some years earlier by a different line of reasoning. He firmly believed that one should not be able to perform any experiment to distinguish between rest and uniform motion. Only the motion of one system relative to another should be detectable. This was his principle of relativity of uniform motion, now called the "Principle of Special Relativity." How could it be made to work for both mechanical experiments and experiments with light? At last it occurred to Einstein that time itself was the problem.

Einstein realized that if there is a limit to the speed at which we can send light signals, then it does not makes sense to talk about events occurring at the same time in different places. Suppose that an observer standing at the side of a road sees lightning strike both ends of a moving train at the same time. An observer standing at the center of the train coach will disagree. Because he is moving toward the point where the lightning struck the front of the coach, he will see *that* flash *before* the flash from the back. Events which the first observer sees happening at the same time in different places do not seem to be happening at the same time for an observer moving relative to the observer at the side of the road. This means that there is no single way to draw a spacetime diagram that reflects what happened.

Understanding that the velocity of light should be the same in both the moving and stationary trains, Einstein was able to work out just how to draw a spacetime diagram. This enables us to have a theory of light which agrees with experiment.

Understanding Time

But we have still not reached the end of the story. The laws of dynamics assumed

According to some sources, Einstein created a humorous illustration so that his secretary could explain the nature of time and his theory of relativity to reporters in a simple way. He told the secretary to answer, "When you sit with a nice girl for two hours you think it's only a minute, but when you sit on a hot stove for a minute you think it's two hours. That's relativity."

that we were able to say what we meant by the same time in different places once and for all. Can Newton's laws, which for 200 years helped unlock the secrets of the universe, be wrong? Yes, they can, because once we have been forced to change our ideas on the nature of time, we cannot unchange them. We must change the laws instead.

Light moves very quickly. In one and a quarter seconds, a pulse of light travels to the moon, a distance of a quarter of a million miles, some ten times the distance around the earth's equator. This, according to Einstein's theory, is the fastest possible speed at which any signal can travel. For the much slower speeds at which we usually travel, Newton's laws are very accurate. In his special theory of relativity, Einstein worked out how they must be modified for very high speeds.

There are many results of these changes of the laws that can be tested in modern experiments. For more than a century, the theory of relativity has withstood these tests. One result, the most famous, is the remarkable finding that energy, or heat, is equivalent to mass, and that they are changeable, one into the other. The light and warmth of the sun, which gives us life, comes from a decrease in its mass. It is the same process that gives us the hydrogen bomb.

One final comment on relative motion: Once it was known that there is no single correct way to draw the vertical lines on our spacetime diagrams, it may not seem such a remarkable step to realize that this was also true of the horizontal lines. It is the nature of great ideas that looking back, they seem so simple and obvious.

In 1905, unknown to Einstein, two other men had already discovered the mathematical ingredients of his theory. One was Henri Poincaré (1854–1912), one of the greatest figures in the history of mathematics in France. The other was Hendrik Lorentz (1853–1928), whom Einstein was later to regard as the leading physicist of his generation. But it was Einstein alone who recognized what mathematics was telling us about the nature of the world; in his own words, "that time itself was suspect."

TEXT-DEPENDENT QUESTIONS

1. What did Einstein and his pupils in Berne, Switzerland, Maurice Solovine and Konrad Habicht, call themselves?
2. What theory did the Austrian physicist Ludwig Boltzmann develop?

RESEARCH PROJECT

Using the internet or your school library, find out more about one of the following scientists who made important contributions to our understanding of time: Isaac Newton, Galileo Galilei, Albert Michelson, Edward Morley, Arthur Eddington, Albert Einstein, Edwin Hubble, or Stephen Hawking. Write a two-page paper that discusses this scientist's accomplishments, and present it to your class.

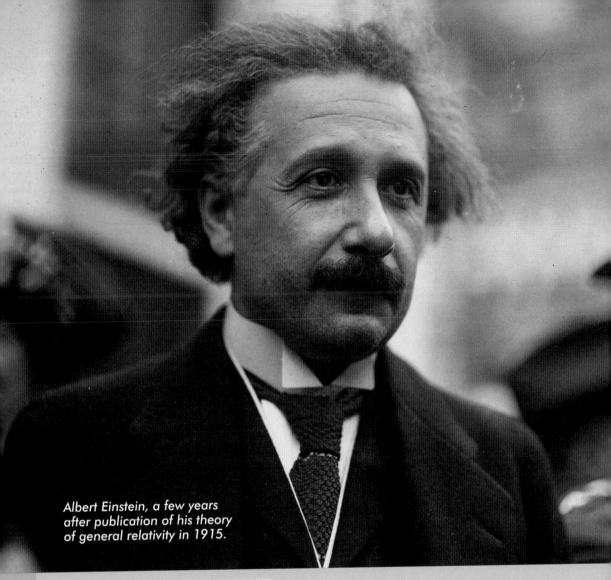

Albert Einstein, a few years after publication of his theory of general relativity in 1915.

WORDS TO UNDERSTAND

eclipse: an eclipse of the sun occurs when the moon passes directly between the earth and the sun. If the eclipse is "total," the moon completely blocks out the light from the sun for a short while. "Partial" eclipses, when the moon obscures only a portion of the sun, occur more frequently, but are less interesting.

Law of Universal Gravitation: a law giving the strength of the force by which any object attracts any other object.

CHAPTER 3

A New Copernicus

In 1906, the year following the publication of his three famous articles, Einstein received a small promotion in the Patents Office. There was no connection between the two events. His superiors in the Civil Service were not aware of his outside work.

However, Einstein's writings had aroused great interest among the leading men of science. Polish physicist August Witowski hailed him as "a new Copernicus." From a Pole, no higher praise was possible than to compare him to the great Polish astronomer of the sixteenth century. Of more importance was the fact that Einstein's articles had attracted the attention of two of the most respected physicists of the time, Max Planck (1858–1947) and Hendrik Lorentz (1853–1928). Planck visited Einstein, and the two men became lifelong friends.

It was natural that Einstein should now seek a university appointment. The custom of the time required that he should first serve as a *privatdozent*. This position meant that he had to lecture at a university, but was not paid a salary. Einstein applied for such a post in Zurich. He was rejected. The essay on relativity that he submitted to support his application was considered to be too short and too complicated. Fortunately the decision was later reversed, but it was not until 1908 that Einstein stepped onto the first rung of the academic ladder, as a *privatdozent* at Berne University.

When a vacancy occurred for a professorship at Zurich University in the following summer, Einstein was a natural candidate. He was by now widely regarded as an important figure in the world of physics. The Board of Education, however, thought differently. A majority of them were Social Democrats, and they favored the appointment of Friedrich Adler, son of the founder of the Austrian Social Democratic Party. But Adler was a generous man, and when he realized this, he immediately refused the post and insisted that it should be given to Einstein. Eventually Einstein was appointed.

Max Planck, founder of the quantum theory and winner of the Nobel Prize for Physics in 1918. The German physicist was an early supporter of Einstein's work.

Einstein never came to regard any one place as his home. He was always eager to move to wherever he thought would most benefit his work. Thus in 1911 he accepted a post at Prague, a first-rate university. In Zurich his wife Mileva had had to take in lodgers to make ends meet. Now Einstein received the full salary of a professor. Now, perhaps, he might have intended to settle down, but even before he had settled in, he was negotiating for a post at his old polytechnic in Zurich. The following summer he returned there.

During these years Einstein had been trying to extend the theory of relativity to include gravitational forces. Gravitation, or gravity, is the name given to the force that causes objects to fall to the ground when dropped. Newton discovered how to calculate this force in his theory of gravitation. Whereas Newton's laws of dynamics could readily be amended to satisfy Einstein's principle of relativity, as we have seen, the **Law of Universal Gravitation** was proving more difficult to change. Einstein had reached an understanding of the basic physical ideas he needed. What he lacked was a satisfactory mathematical theory.

There now occurred a remarkable coincidence. At Zurich Polytechnic was Marcel Grossmann, the same man who had helped Einstein pass his examinations, and who had helped him to get a job at the Patents Office in Berne. By now, Grossmann had become a specialist in that very field of mathematics that Einstein found he needed to complete his theory of gravitation. Einstein's attitude to mathematics is revealed in a letter to a colleague:

> I am now exclusively occupied with the problem of gravitation and hope to overcome all the difficulties. Never in life have I been quite so tormented. A great respect for mathematics has been instilled in me, the subtler aspects of which, in my stupidity, I regarded until now as pure luxury. Compared with the problem of gravitation, the original problem of the theory of relativity is child's play.

By 1914 he still did not have his theory, but he had mastered the mathematical methods. Max Planck arranged for him to receive a professorship in Berlin, then the center of European science. In Berlin, Einstein had no official duties and could devote all his energies to research. For once, even Einstein was not completely

EINSTEIN'S THEORY OF HAPPINESS

In October 2017, a brief note written by Albert Einstein sold at an auction house in Jerusalem for more than $1.5 million. Einstein had written the notes while visiting Tokyo to lecture in 1922, shortly after learning he had won the Nobel Prize for Physics. While there, a messenger had delivered something to his hotel room, but Einstein did not have money for a tip. He instead wrote and signed a note for the messenger, on stationary of the Imperial Hotel in Tokyo. The note contained one sentence, in German, which read, "A calm and humble life will bring more happiness than the pursuit of success and the constant restlessness that comes with it." He told the messenger that if he was lucky, the note would become valuable.

confident. "The Germans are betting on me as a prize hen; I am myself not sure whether I am going to lay another egg," he wrote to a friend.

Einstein was to remain in Berlin until driven out of Germany by the war twenty years later, but his wife returned to Zurich almost immediately. Their marriage had not been a happy one. They could be friends as long as they did not have to live together. For Einstein, struggling with his equations, it was better that they separated. There was a last, disastrous meeting between the couple in 1916, and the final break came with divorce in 1919. In 1922, when Einstein received the Nobel Prize in Physics, the highest award in science, the money he received was earmarked to support Mileva and their two sons.

Disruption of War

August 1914 saw the outbreak of the First World War. In the patriotic frenzy that on both sides urged young men to the misery of death in the trenches, many of Einstein's colleagues in Berlin turned their energies to the German war effort. For example, Fritz Haber (1868–1934), the director of the Chemistry Institute in

French soldiers use flamethrowers against attacking Germans on the front line of a battle-field. Einstein hated the destruction of war, and worked hard to try to prevent it.

English astronomer Sir Arthur Eddington (1882–1944) introduced the general theory of relativity to the English-speaking world. In 1919 he led the first experiment to test the theory by measuring the bending of light rays by the sun.

Berlin, led the development of poisonous gases. Haber is known as the "father of chemical warfare" for his work in developing chlorine, a toxic gas used against British and French troops at the Second Battle of Ypres, Belgium, in April 1915. Einstein was one of a few German scientists who opposed the war. He continued with his work as the war engulfed Europe and spread to battlefields throughout the world.

Finally, in 1916 Einstein formed his theory of gravitation, which he called the "General Theory of Relativity." In this he was helped by his research on the behavior of light. He had suspected for several years that light rays bend as they pass close to the sun. Now he could calculate a definite value for the amount of bending. This value was compared with the value that might be worked out from the Theory of Universal Gravitation put forward by Isaac Newton two centuries earlier. Einstein's value was twice as large.

The article containing Einstein's theory of gravitation found its way to English astronomer Arthur Eddington (1882–1944) in 1917. Eddington was immediately impressed, and began planning an experiment that would prove Einstein's theory. Even though Britain and Germany were on opposite sides of the Great War, as the ongoing conflict was known, the British government granted funds for Eddington's proposed expedition.

Eddington knew that in 1919, there would be a total **eclipse** of the sun. He reasoned that during the eclipse, it would be possible for photographs to be taken of stars near the sun. These could be compared with photographs of the same stars when the sun was not present, and the different positions of the stars on the photographs would help researchers understand how much bending of light occurred.

In the same year, Einstein had suffered a breakdown in Berlin. Exhaustion from overwork, from the tension of the war, and from his lack of attention to his health, had caught up with him. Throughout his illness he was looked after by his cousin Elsa. When the divorce from Mileva was confirmed in 1919, Elsa became Einstein's wife.

Meanwhile, in Principe, a small island off the west coast of Africa, Eddington and his colleague Edwin Turner Cottingham (1869–1940) had succeeded in taking photographs of the eclipse. Before the expedition had left England, Cottingham asked the Royal Astronomer, Sir Frank Dyson (1868–1939), what would happen if the results showed twice the Einstein prediction. "Then Eddington will go mad and you will have to come home alone," Sir Frank replied. As he measured the first photographic plate, Eddington turned to his colleague and said; "Cottingham, you won't have to go home alone." Einstein's prediction had been correct.

The success of the expedition was relayed to Einstein in a telegram. He was pleased, of course, although he had never been in any doubt about the outcome. Now his general theory of relativity had been proved in practice. On November 5, 1919, Eddington announced the results to a packed meeting of the Royal Astronomical Society. The response was immediate. Following the newspaper accounts of the meeting, Einstein's home was besieged by reporters. He had become a world figure.

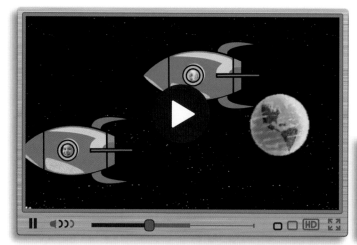

Scan here for a a short video explaining Einstein's theory of relativity:

The Fabric of the Universe

The great twentieth century English physicist Paul Dirac (1902–84) called Einstein's theory of general relativity "probably the greatest scientific discovery that was ever made," because it was so unexpected. The theory captured the imagination of scientist and non-scientist alike. It was revealed to a world eager to forget war. It concerned the mysteries of space and time. If not everyone could understand the theory, they could at least sense the mysteries.

In order to construct his theory, Einstein started from a definite theoretical problem that arose between his theory of special relativity and Isaac Newton's older laws of motion and universal gravitation. Both agreed that gravitational attraction between the earth and the sun keeps the earth in orbit around the sun. According to Newton's laws, if the sun were suddenly to disappear, the earth would immediately fly off into space. However, if the special theory of relativity is correct, no signal or force—including the gravitational force—can travel faster than the speed of light. It takes about eight minutes for light to travel from the sun to the earth, so if the sun suddenly disappeared, Einstein reasoned, it should take at least eight minutes

Einstein and his second wife, Elsa, during a visit to Washington, DC, in the early 1920s.

before the earth starts to fly off into space. Therefore Newton's laws and Einstein's theory cannot both be strictly correct.

In his search for the solution to this problem, Einstein was led back to the works of Austrian physicist Ernst Mach (1838–1916). Einstein had read Mach as a young man and had been deeply impressed. Mach had also been dissatisfied with

Austrian physicist Ernst Mach (1838–1916) believed that space and time only have meaning when the results of their relationship can actually be seen. He had a great influence on Einstein's early work on relativity.

Newton's law. He had argued that one should be able to observe only the motion of one object *relative* to another. It should never be possible to say which object is "really" moving and which is "really" at rest, and it should not make any difference whether that motion is uniform or not. Newton's law does not have this property. Nor does Einstein's Principle of Special Relativity, for it applies only to uniform motion.

Einstein thought up a simple example. Most of us have had the experience of going up to the top of a tall building in an elevator. As long as the elevator is moving steadily, without any bumps or change in speed, there is no way of telling whether it is really moving or not. However, if the elevator comes to a sudden halt, we feel ourselves jerked upward as if we were suddenly lighter. If the lift begins to rise again, we feel ourselves dragged downward. It seems as if we can quite easily tell when the motion is not uniform.

To understand that this is not so, imagine an elevator in outer space, far removed from the influence of the earth. Inside is a cooperative scientist who has not been told where he is, and cannot see out of the elevator. As long as the elevator gathers speed, he feels himself pulled downward, just as we did in our earthbound elevator. Just as we might think that a moving elevator is in fact at rest, so the scientist might think that he is still at rest on the earth, feeling its gravitational pull.

We now ask our scientist to do a simple experiment. He is to drop two objects of unequal weight, say a feather and a brick, at the same time, and observe when they hit the floor of the lift. He reports that they hit the floor at the same time. We are not surprised. We see that the objects, once released, continue to move at the same speed as when they were dropped, until the floor of the lift, rising faster and faster, comes up and hits them. Does this convince the scientist that he is not at rest on the earth? It does not. In fact it confirms his opinion. For he knows that, according to legend, Galileo dropped two stones, one large, one small, from the leaning tower of Pisa, and saw that they hit the ground at the same time. It is a property of gravity that heavier objects do not fall faster than lighter objects. Is there any experiment we can ask the scientist to do to convince him of his error? Einstein's answer was no. Any variation from uniformity of motion in the absence of gravity can always be interpreted as the effect of gravity in the absence of motion.

Einstein called this the "Principle of Equivalence." It was the first major result of his investigations into general relativity.

Let us now return to our spacetime diagrams. Up to now our lines have all been straight. Straight lines represent motion at constant speed, as they did in the spacetime diagrams of the train experiments. Non-uniform motion is represented by a curved line. Suppose that we draw our spacetime diagrams on a rubber sheet. Then we can stretch the sheet so that any one line becomes straight, no matter how curved it was to start with. In particular the sheet can be pulled so that any line previously curved is now vertical, and so represents a body at rest. In this way we can draw spacetime diagrams in which all motion is relative, because on our rubber sheet, any line, straight or curved, can be regarded as representing an object at rest. In our diagram, the lines that were straight on the unstretched rubber are dotted, so that we do not lose track of them.

This is not yet quite the true picture. We have agreed that in the real world, we cannot say what we mean by true uniform motion. We cannot tell which bodies travel on dotted lines, so we do not know how to draw them in. We do not know when the rubber is unstretched and when it is stretched. Another way of saying this is that we cannot pretend that gravity does not exist and find out how bodies would move without it, because there is no known way of shielding bodies from the effects of gravity. The best we can do is to shield them from all other influences. Therefore it is more sensible to draw with dotted lines the motion of objects moving under gravity only.

We must try to find a convenient way of drawing the spacetime diagram so that we can tell where the dotted lines should be in any situation. To illustrate how this is done, let us imagine a map of the world's airline routes. On a map showing where the aircraft really travel, these routes are not straight lines. They are more complicated than they need be, because aircraft have to avoid flying over countries with hostile governments and flying through bad air currents, but suppose we ignore these influences. Then the routes will be the shortest distances between any two cities. To make things simple, pretend that all aircraft travel at the same speed over the ground. Then we can construct the routes once we know the takeoff and landing times of the aircraft. Now most of the routes on the map are still not straight lines. However we stretch or squash the map, we cannot make all of them straight at the same time. This is because the surface of earth is not really flat, like the map, but curved.

In Einstein's theory, we make a space-travel timetable of the universe instead of an air-travel timetable of the earth. Einstein's calculations tell us how to do this.

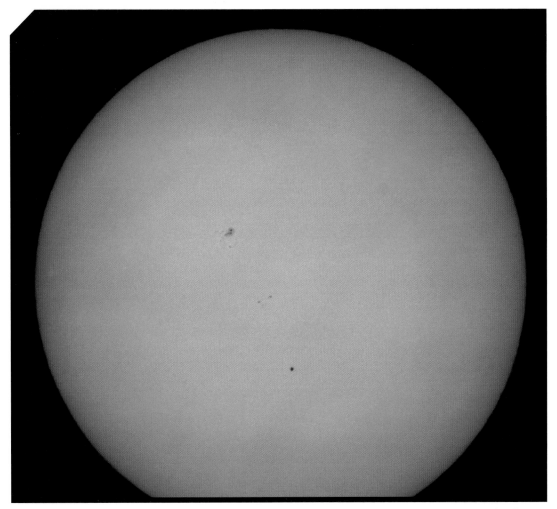

The planet Mercury is seen in silhouette, lower center of image, as it moves across the face of the sun. Mercury passes between Earth and the sun only about thirteen times a century, most recently in 2016, with the previous pass taking place in 2006. The movement of Mercury was an instance where Einstein's new theory was more accurate than Newton's laws of the motion of the planets.

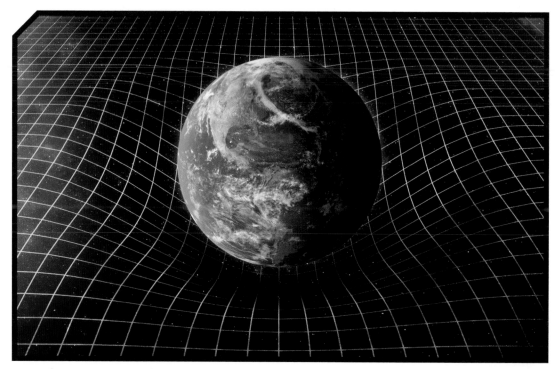

According to Einstein's theory of general relativity, the phenomenon that Newton called "gravity" is actually caused by the curvature of spacetime around objects with mass, including planets like Earth, stars like our Sun, and other objects in the universe.

From the timetable we can construct the motions of bodies under gravity alone, represented by the dotted lines. This is the objective of a theory of gravity. We can do this no matter how the spacetime diagram is stretched, just as we can draw airline routes on any projection of the earth's surface.

In carrying this out, Einstein made a remarkable discovery. He found that it is impossible to make all the dotted lines straight at once. Any single one, yes. But not all of them at once, as long as gravity is acting. This is just what we found with the map of airline routes. We describe it in the same way, by saying that spacetime is curved in the presence of gravity. It was the second main result of Einstein's theory.

In order to formulate a theory of gravity that would not contradict the principles of the special theory of relativity, Einstein had to extend that theory. If gravitational fields are present, we have to draw our spacetime diagrams in a new way. This is the reason for the names "special" and "general," as applied to relativity. If objects are moving slowly and gravitational forces are weak, Newton's theory of gravitation is a satisfactory approximate theory. In other situations, Einstein's theory must be used. One such situation is the bending of light rays by the sun. This was a new effect that had not been observed before.

There was another mystery, known for a long time, which had not been explained by the old laws. The planet Mercury did not move as Newton's theory said it should. Every century, Mercury had moved just seven-sixths of one-hundredth of a degree too far around the sun. When Einstein calculated the motion of Mercury according to his theory, he found just such an extra motion. It is hardly surprising then, that he was in little doubt about the outcome of Eddington's eclipse expedition.

 TEXT-DEPENDENT QUESTIONS

1.   What influential German physicist arranged for Einstein to receive a professorship in Berlin in 1914?

2.   What British astronomer carried out an experiment that would prove Einstein's theory of relativity?

 RESEARCH PROJECT

Read the article "The Eclipse that Revealed the Universe," which provides details about the 1919 expedition that affirmed Einstein's theory of general relativity. The article can be found at https://www.nytimes.com/2017/07/31/science/eclipse-einstein-general-relativity.html.

CHAPTER 4

A Famous Name

Neither before nor since has any theoretical scientist achieved such world fame as Einstein did in the years following the eclipse expedition in 1919. Journalists were eager for interviews and stories. Hundreds of books were written trying to explain the meaning of relativity. Wherever Einstein traveled, the public flocked to see him. Whenever he lectured, halls were filled by people who could not have understood him, but who wanted to get a glimpse of the man who had revolutionized science.

Fame was the last thing that Einstein had expected—and the last thing he wanted. It disturbed the peace he needed for his work. Sometimes it amused him. When asked by someone who did not recognize him what he did, he thought of the number of times people had wanted to draw his picture. "I am an artists' model," he joked.

In the following, years his demeanor changed from the arrogant young man that he had been at school to a more serene and humble figure. For fame brought to Einstein an overwhelming sense of responsibility. If people listened when he spoke, then it followed that he had a duty to speak up for what he believed to be right. He was willing to put his name to any cause he believed to be good. He did this so often that it began to work against him. So many foreign students came to England in the 1930s with a recommendation from Albert Einstein that they were advised not to bother mentioning the fact to university examination boards!

Einstein had become involved in politics during the First World War. It is hard to understand today, but at the outbreak of war in 1914, many people in both Britain and Germany welcomed the conflict out of a sense of national pride. Only later, as the war dragged on and millions of young men died or were wounded on the front

Piles of German money in a Berlin bank during the post-World War I hyperinflation. In Germany, money became worth very little, and huge amounts were needed just to buy food. Many peoples' savings were quickly wiped out.

lines, did people's attitudes change. Einstein hated the war from the outset, and joined a German political party dedicated to ending the war as soon as possible. He took part in anti-war demonstrations, and encouraged people to refuse to join the armed forces when they were called up. Einstein believed that even if only a small number of men practiced this sort of **civil disobedience**, it would become impossible for governments to wage wars.

Along with his pacifism, when the First World War ended, Einstein also became involved in a second major cause: establishing better relations between the nations of the world.

Traveling the World

In June 1919, at the Paris peace conference that officially ended World War I, the victorious Allied Powers (particularly Great Britain, France, Italy, and the United States) imposed harsh conditions on the defeated Germans and their allies. The German economy crumbled under the strain. Although Einstein was hard-pressed financially, he was well-off compared to most people. For many Germans this period of inflation brought complete ruin and poverty. These conditions reawakened Einstein's feelings of being German, and in 1920, he voluntarily became a German citizen again.

In the summer of 1921 Einstein made his first visit to England. In a country where, a few years earlier, dachshunds had been killed because they were German dogs, and "German" had become a term of abuse, it was not clear how he would be received. From his first public lecture in Manchester, however, it was clear that Einstein's visit was going to be a success. A modest, quiet man gently explaining the mysteries of the universe quickly won the hearts of those who heard him. His visit did much to improve postwar relations between Britain and Germany.

Einstein traveled widely in the years between the wars. He visited America, Japan, and most of Western Europe. The main aim of these visits was usually to explain his theories, or to hear what others had to say about them. But the cause of better relations between governments and peoples cannot have been entirely absent from his mind.

A further purpose of his travels was the support of Zionism. This was a movement that began in the nineteenth century, dedicated to creating a new country in the region of the Middle East known as Palestine that would be a homeland for the Jewish people. In 1919 Einstein was persuaded to take part in a fundraising tour in the United States. The money from the tour was to be used to establish a Hebrew University in Palestine, a project in which he took an active interest.

In the United States, however, Einstein was not universally popular. Some Americans suspected him of holding left-wing views, of not believing in God, and of being a pacifist. As a result, his visits had to be handled with care to avoid these delicate issues.

In science Einstein was the undisputed master. But the qualities that brought him such success in science held him back in political action. In physics he had the instinct to go to the heart of a problem and logically work out the solution. The political art is different, because men do not behave according to the rules of logic. Einstein was never a master of tact. Nor had he the patience or the cunning to take part in political dealings. In physics his depth of thought was beyond most men. Outside his chosen sphere, he could appear to possess no more wisdom than the average man. He followed his conscience in using his one asset, the power of his name. Where this alone would not lead to success, more often than not he failed.

Scan here to learn how Einstein's "biggest blunder" might not have been a mistake after all:

EINSTEIN AND RELIGION

Although Albert Einstein's parents were Jewish, he was not a practicing Jew. Einstein had read the Hebrew Bible as a child, but generally rejected its stories about God when he was about twelve years old because these stories did not fit in with his scientific understanding of the world. He would later call the stories in the Hebrew Bible "primitive legends" and "superstitions."

Just because Einstein did not practice Judaism does not mean that he didn't believe in God. He rejected the idea that God takes a personal interest in the activities of humans, however. Einstein explained that he did not believe the world could be explained solely in scientific terms. Certainly one could scientifically analyze a piece of music. But there was more to the music than that. One could call that extra element "God," and Einstein often did.

Einstein believed that humans could not understand God, but that God could be seen in terms of the beauty and unity of the universe. "The most beautiful emotion we can experience is the mysterious," Einstein wrote in 1930. "It is the fundamental emotion that stands at the cradle of all true art and science. He to whom this emotion is a stranger, who can no longer wonder and stand rapt in awe, is as good as dead, a snuffed-out candle. To sense that behind anything that can be experienced there is something that our minds cannot grasp, whose beauty and sublimity reaches us only indirectly: this is religiousness. In this sense, and in this sense only, I am a devoutly religious man."

Thought not a devout Jew, Einstein felt a deep bond with the Jewish people. He believed that Jews shared an ability to face the world with awe and joy, as well as a sense of social justice. Like other Jews in Europe, he regularly experienced anti-Semitism. This led him to support the Zionist movement to establish a homeland for Jews in Palestine.

A Picture of the World

For all his political activities, it was science that came first and second for Einstein. A colleague once said of him, "He could talk about physics with as much ease as if he were discussing the weather." Having proposed the theory of general relativity, he did not sit back and listen to the applause. Instead, he went on to apply the theory on the largest possible scale—to the structure of the universe as a whole. We call this study "cosmology." It has been a subject of discussion since the beginning of thought itself. With Einstein, it became a science.

The aim of cosmology is to draw a picture of the universe in which we live, leaving out of the picture what are considered to be unnecessary details. Such a picture is called a "model." A model does not have to tell us where each and every individual star is. If it did, it would be far too complicated to understand. We ask only that certain overall features be correctly shown. We might ask, for example, approximately how many stars are there? Or, do they cluster together in groups? Or, does their motion show any general pattern? It is like taking a census of the population of a country. We might be interested in whether there is a drift of population from the country to the towns, or what the average size of a family is. We are not interested in the detailed habits of a particular person.

The main force controlling the motion of the stars is gravity. Let us see what happens if we try to apply Newton's theory of gravity to the whole universe. Suppose the universe were infinite; that is, never ending. Then, our model must be so sparsely populated with stars that there would be fewer and fewer stars as we go further out from the center. It seems unlikely that the real universe is like this, since there is no evidence for this thinning out as we look further away. So this is not a good model. On the other hand, if the universe were finite, that is, if it came to an end, then Newton's theory says that all the stars must fall toward the center, drawn in by gravity. As we know, this does not happen.

In the bending of light rays, and the motion of the planet Mercury, we saw that Einstein's theory is superior to Newton's. So it is in cosmology. In 1917 Einstein discovered that the difficulties of making a model according to Newtonian theory did not appear to arise in general relativity. He found that he could construct a model in which space is finite but curved. We can represent it as a cylinder. That

Jewish students attend a class at the Einstein Institute for Mathematics at Hebrew University in Jerusalem, late 1920s. Einstein was one of the founders of the university, and served as a member of the university's Board of Governors when it opened in 1925. Einstein also left his scientific and non-scientific writings, as well as the rights to his works, to the university after his death.

Hot stars burn brightly in this image of the Andromeda galaxy, which is approximately 2.5 million light-years away from our galaxy, the Milky Way, and is our largest neighbor. Scientists believe the Andromeda galaxy is similar in appearance to the Milky Way. Our sun is just one of the millions of stars in the Milky Way galaxy.

is, our spacetime diagram is drawn onto a sheet of paper, which is wrapped around and its edges glued together. We must imagine that the cylinder is infinitely long; its ends extend without limit. This is because, in the model, the universe lasts forever; time has no beginning and no end. According to Einstein's model, however, if you were to set out on a journey into space, you would not come to the edge of the universe, nor would you be able to travel forever through new regions of space. After a very long time, you would come back to your starting point.

Einstein's model has the important feature that, on average, nothing changes. There is no drift of stars in one direction rather than another. There is no increase or decrease in the number of stars in any region.

Mysteries of the Universe

Does this model provide anything like a true picture of the universe? To find out, we shall have to look at what the universe is seen to be like.

Clustered around the sun are eight planets (including the earth) and five **dwarf planets**. The planets in our solar system do not shine by their own light, but by the reflected light of the sun. The sun is a rather ordinary star among a vast group of stars called the "galaxy," or the Milky Way. To get an idea of how many stars there are in the galaxy, imagine counting them at a rate of one per second. Then the whole of the recorded history of mankind up to the present day would just give enough time to complete the count. To get an idea of the size of the galaxy, imagine it to be possible to travel to Pluto, the planet furthest away from us in the solar system, in one hour. Then it would take four years to travel to the nearest star in the galaxy. To travel across the galaxy would take 75,000 years. Continue the journey beyond the galaxy for another million years, and you would come to another, similar group of stars, called the Andromeda galaxy. Our galaxy and the Andromeda galaxy are just two in a larger cluster of galaxies called the Virgo Supercluster. In the whole of the universe that we can see from the earth, there are hundreds of millions of other clusters. On average, each cluster contains 100 galaxies. Now you have an idea of just how big the universe is.

But the most amazing feature of the universe is not its size. Rather, it is the discovery made in 1929 by Edwin Hubble (1889–1953) that the galaxies appear

This rare galaxy cluster, which is located 10 billion light-years from Earth, was observed using the Hubble Space Telescope. The telescope is named for astronomer Edwin Hubble, who in 1929 discovered that the galaxies are all moving away from each other—our universe is expanding.

to be moving away from each other. The further away a galaxy is from us, the faster it appears to be moving away from us. In other words, the universe is expanding.

To understand this, imagine a balloon with dots painted on it, each dot representing a galaxy. As the balloon is blown up, all the dots get further away from each other. The balloon is expanding, but there is no particular dot that can be said to be at the center.

The expansion of the universe means that Einstein's model must be wrong, for as noted previously, it was based on the idea of an unchanging, static universe. Einstein himself immediately recognized and admitted his error.

Einstein's theory of general relativity actually works when describing an expanding universe. But the idea of a static, or unchanging, universe was the accepted scientific belief at the time Einstein created his model. When Einstein applied his equations to a static universe, they did not work. They indicated that a static universe would be unstable and collapse upon itself. So Einstein added a hypothetical force, which he called the "cosmological constant," to balance things out and fix the problem. Had he trusted his calculations instead, Einstein could have been able to predict that the universe was expanding. Changing his calculations so that they would fit a preconceived idea, he would later say, was "the biggest blunder of my life."

 TEXT-DEPENDENT QUESTIONS

1. What is civil disobedience?
2. What is Zionism?
3. What surprising discovery about the universe did Edwin Hubble make in 1929?

 RESEARCH PROJECT

Watch the short movie "From the Big Bang to the LHC" (available at http://education.web.cern.ch/education/Chapter2/Teaching/from-the-big-bang-to-lhc/Globe-movie-l.mp4) to find out more about the Big Bang and the origins of space and time.

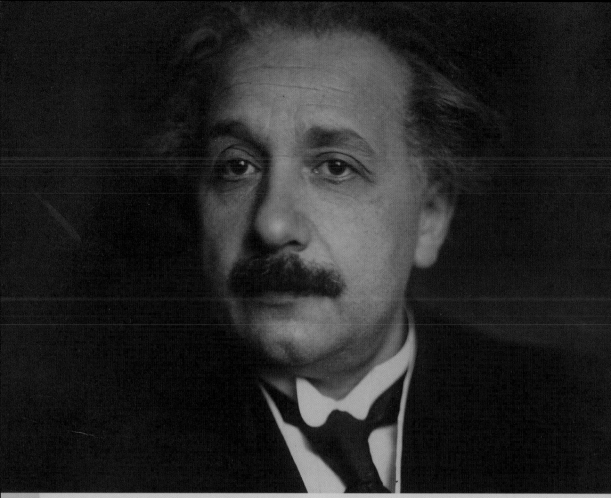

WORDS TO UNDERSTAND

atomic nucleus: small central region of an atom containing most of its mass.

electron: sub-atomic particle carrying one unit of electric charge.

probability: in tossing a coin one cannot tell whether it will fall heads or tails, but there is a probability of one half that it will be heads. Certain events occurring by chance like this are nonetheless subject to laws. One cannot say what will happen on a particular occasion, but one can say how often a particular outcome should be expected.

quantum: the smallest unit of light (or heat) that can be absorbed or emitted by an object.

sub—atomic: building blocks of matter smaller than atoms.

CHAPTER 5

$P = mv$

$E = mc^2$

$E_k = \dfrac{m}{}$

$W =$

To America

Science usually progresses in small steps. A particular problem requires a particular insight for its solution. Usually the insight is within the bounds of existing theories, and if the result agrees with experiment the solution is accepted. Occasionally it appears to be impossible to solve a problem within the existing theory. It is then that a new theory must be formed. Such a new theory will be accepted if the ideas expressed are simple and beautiful. It must also make predictions that are later confirmed by experiment.

By 1919, Einstein's theory of relativity was generally considered to have passed those tests, but not everyone agreed. Some scientists did not find his ideas simple and beautiful, because they could not understand the theory in terms of the rules of physics they were used to. Others, failing to understand the new ideas, found themselves left behind. They did not like this, and so they hoped the theory was wrong. To a small handful of scientists, whether they understood the theory or not, relativity suffered from one major fault—it was invented by a Jew. In the anti-Semitic atmosphere of Germany between the two World Wars, such a movement could soon find supporters.

An anti-Einstein movement was founded in 1919. One of its leading members, Philipp Lenard (1862–1947), was himself a winner of the Nobel Prize. In the eyes of the public, this lent the movement a certain respectability. Anti-Einstein articles were published, and public meetings were held to condemn the theory of relativity. At one of these meetings, where Einstein was supposed to have the chance to reply to criticisms, there were organized interruptions, and armed police were present to prevent violence.

During the early 1930s, many Germans were angry about the country's high rates of infla-tion and unemployment. These economic problems—made worse by a worldwide depres-sion that began in 1929—created conditions in which Adolf Hitler and his National Socialist German Workers' (Nazi) Party could gain power. Hitler promised a better life for all Germans, as well as a new and glorious state. After the Nazi Party won a large number of seats in the German legislature (the Reichstag) in 1932, Hitler became the chancellor, or head of the government, in January 1933.

Indeed, violence was not completely unlikely. In 1922, Einstein had to cancel a lecture because public appearances were dangerous. In November of the following year, Adolf Hitler led an armed uprising in Munich, Germany. Fearing general disturbances, Einstein left Germany for a time until the uprising was suppressed and Hitler imprisoned.

On March 14, 1929, Einstein's fiftieth birthday, he received congratulations from all over the world. The German chancellor, Hermann Müller, spoke in his honor. A German laborer sent him an ounce of tobacco. Not everyone celebrated, however. The "anti-relativity company" produced a book called *100 Authors Against Einstein*. Einstein commented, "If I were wrong, then one would have been enough."

Scan here to learn more about atoms:

Rise of the Nazis in Germany

Although Einstein was always committed to his work, he was also aware of the changing attitudes in Germany. He began to establish links with American and British universities, where he could continue his work if he had to leave Germany. In January 1933, while Einstein was visiting the California Institute of Technology, the Nazi Party had gained power through elections and Adolf Hitler became the chancellor of Germany. By March of 1933, Hitler had become virtually a dictator and the reign of Nazi terror had begun. Einstein announced that he would not

A pedestrian walks past a Jewish-owned printing business in Berlin. The windows were smashed during kristallnacht, the "Night of Broken Glass," November 1938. The Nazi regime encouraged such attacks on German Jews after coming to power in 1933. Einstein left Germany, never to return, because of the government's attitude toward Jews.

Belgium's King Albert I and Queen Elisabeth (left) walk with King Fouad I during a visit to Egypt in 1930. Einstein became close friends with the king and queen, and worked with them to try to avert the Second World War, and later to prevent the use of the atomic bomb.

go back to Germany. "I shall live only in a country where civil liberty, tolerance, and equality of all citizens before the law prevail. These conditions do not exist in Germany at the present time." A Berlin newspaper announced "Good news from Einstein—he's not coming back."

To reinforce the message, Einstein was unofficially warned by the German consul in New York not to return to Germany. Shortly afterward his house in Germany was raided by the Nazi militia, and his bank account was confiscated.

On April 1, 1933, the Nazi government passed laws that prohibited Jews from holding any official positions, including teaching at universities. Ultimately 1,600 lecturers who were suspected of being Jewish, or of having Jewish relatives, were dismissed. Fritz Haber, who had led the German research into chemical warfare in the First World War and who had previously converted to Christianity along with his entire family, was one of many who were forced to resign his professorship. Haber was not even allowed to serve his few remaining months to retirement. Heartbroken, he died alone, on his way to Jerusalem. Protests against the new laws were futile. Internationally renowned physicist Max Planck, who spoke publicly in support of Einstein, was told later by Hitler that only his age had kept him from a concentration camp. From outside Germany all that could be done was to provide help for the refugees who managed to escape. Many of Germany's leading scientists fled—a loss that Hitler would later regret.

From America, Einstein traveled with his wife to the little seaside town of Le Coq-sur-mer in Belgium, where he was protected by two bodyguards. That summer, he was summoned urgently to Brussels for a meeting with the Belgian king. Einstein had first met King Albert in 1929 when he had visited the royal palace in Brussels. During this visit he performed chamber music with Queen Elizabeth and enjoyed a supper of spinach, eggs, and boiled potatoes. Now the king sought Einstein's views on the problem of conscientious objectors—men who, on the grounds of their conscience, refused to do military service. In the past, Einstein, as a pacifist, had encouraged such actions. Shortly after the meeting with the king of Belgium, Einstein published a letter renouncing his pacifism in present circumstances. He argued that the only way to resist the threat from Hitler's Germany was by force.

Ernest Rutherford (1871–1937), a physicist from New Zealand, discovered the nucleus and identified the parts of atoms. Einstein called him, "One of the greatest experimental scientists of all time."

Founded in 1930 by Abraham Flexner, the postdoctoral research center Institute for Advanced Study is located in the woods on Einstein Drive in Princeton, New Jersey.

"Were I a Belgian," he wrote, "I would enter [military] service cheerfully in the belief that I should thereby be helping to save European civilization."

In England, Winston Churchill (1874–1965) was a lonely voice trying to awaken the country to the dangers of Nazism. Einstein visited him to discuss the Nazi menace. Later, in 1933, he spoke at a meeting at the Albert Hall in London, in aid of German refugees. Since the British government thought that to upset Hitler might do more harm than good, no reference to Germany was permitted at the meeting.

On October 7, 1933, Einstein left Europe for the last time. He was bound for the Institute of Advanced Study at Princeton, New Jersey, where he was to spend the rest of his life.

Changing Focus of Work

On December 20, 1936, Einstein's second wife, Elsa, died after a long illness. His escape from his grief was in his work. By now he was no longer part of the mainstream of physics. Relativity had become part of history. Einstein and his assistants produced some important new results in this area, but he was becoming more interested in other fields. To see how he had parted company with most of the scientific community, we must return to the first of those three articles of 1905, and discover what it contained.

In all substances there is an electric charge, positive and negative, like in an electric battery. When a beam of light shines on certain metals, the negative electric charges are emitted from the metal, which is left with a small positive charge. The negative charges are small **sub–atomic** particles (particles smaller than atoms), called **electrons**. The stronger the light, the larger the number of electrons emitted by the metal. The bluer the light, the faster those electrons travel. This is called the "photo-electric effect."

The accepted view of light at the beginning of the 1900s was that it consisted of waves. This was because the mathematical laws that governed the behavior of light were like those that govern the motion of waves on the sea. According to this "wave theory" of light, the stronger the light shining on the metal, the faster

Einstein with three other Nobel Prize-winning nuclear physicists. From left to right: Danish physicist Niels Bohr, who made important discoveries about the structure of the atom; James Franck, a German who studied electrons within the atom; Einstein; and Jewish American Isidor Isaac Rabi, whose discoveries included nuclear magnetic resonance.

the emitted electrons should travel; the bluer the light, the larger the number of electrons that should be emitted. It is just the wrong way around!

At the turn of the century, Max Planck had found that certain properties of light could only be explained if light was thought of as made up of tiny particles. These particles he called "quanta." Einstein, in his 1905 article, showed how this idea could be used to explain the photo-electric effect.

To explain the behavior of light we seem to need two theories. The first theory, that light consists of waves, tells us how it travels from place to place; the second theory, that light consists of particles, tells us how it affects atoms and electrons. Neither theory can be wrong, but both cannot be right. It was Einstein's work that was to suggest to others a way out of the difficulty. To understand how, we need to know something about atoms.

Understanding the Atom

The experiments of Ernest Rutherford (1871–1937) in 1911 had shown that atoms themselves are made of simpler things. There is a central solid region, called the **atomic nucleus**. Around this electrons revolve, like planets revolve around the sun.

Unfortunately, this picture of the atom does not fit in with Maxwell's laws of electricity. According to these, the electron should spiral in to the center of the atom, emitting light as it does so. Therefore, according to Maxwell's theory, atoms cannot exist.

Niels Bohr (1885–1962) discovered a way out of this difficulty. By assuming that light consists of quanta, as Planck had said, he found that an electron cannot spiral in, but can only jump from one orbit to another. The electron cannot emit light as a continuous wave, a little bit at a time, but must emit a whole **quantum** in one go. Bohr found that there was a lowest orbit beyond which the electron cannot fall. A normal atom exists with all the electrons in their lowest orbits.

If a light quantum hits an atom in this normal state, the quantum can be absorbed, and the electron jumps to a new orbit. Suppose the atom is now left completely undisturbed. Will the electron fall back to its old orbit of its own accord? There is no apparent reason why it should. Einstein discovered that in fact it must. But the laws of physics could not tell him how long it would take before a particular electron fell back. Physics could only say that one length of time was more likely than another.

The occurrence of events by chance, for no apparent reason, is common in everyday life. For example, if a light bulb fails, we say that we knew it would do so sooner or later. We do not ask why it failed exactly when it did. But a physicist knows why. Given the knowledge of its manufacture, he could calculate exactly when the bulb will fail.

With the behavior of the electron, the physicist comes up against a new problem. It is never possible, by any means whatsoever, to know enough about the electron to say exactly when it will jump. He can calculate only probabilities. The difference between these problems is only one of size. In finding out about the light bulb filament, we would have to be careful not to break it. With the electron, it is so small that it is impossible to be careful enough not to disturb it.

Einstein himself had unveiled the idea of **probability** as a way around the need for two theories of light. The idea was taken up by others and was found to work. A whole new physics, called "quantum physics," was developed to calculate the probabilities of events in the sub-atomic world. It was here that Einstein disagreed with his colleagues. He could never accept the change from certainty to probability. But as all his arguments against the new physics were demolished, he could only express a belief that "God does not play dice."

Perhaps there was a more fundamental theory that could go beyond quantum physics and its probabilities. Gravity had been related to geometry, in the curvature of spacetime. Perhaps all physics could be related to geometry. At first, Einstein dismissed the idea, but by the time he arrived in Princeton, it was his main hope for an alternative to quantum physics. He would spend the rest of his life working on that hope.

After thirty years, that work was to end in failure. Einstein had regarded it as necessary that the attempt should be made. So small were the chances of succeeding that it could be done only by someone who had no longer to worry about success. Einstein knew that at the institute in Princeton, he was widely regarded as "a historic relic" and an "old fool." In 1921, he had written, "Discovery in the grand manner is for young people … and hence for me a thing of the past." The prophecy was to cast its shadow over his later years. But Einstein, if anyone, had earned the right to one failure.

Today, progress toward unity in physics is being made not through geometry, but through quantum physics One theory stands aloof from quantum physics— Einstein's theory of gravity. We know that the two theories must be brought together. After decades of work, we do not yet know how.

TEXT-DEPENDENT QUESTIONS

1. Why did Einstein decide to leave Germany in 1933?
2. What is the photo-electric effect?
3. What is quantum physics?

RESEARCH PROJECT

Using your school library or the internet, do some research on quantum physics. Explain what you have learned in a two-page paper, and share it with your class.

WORDS TO UNDERSTAND

atomic power (or nuclear power): energy obtained by splitting a heavy atomic nucleus into lighter fragments.

unified field theory: a theory which attempts to derive all physics from geometry.

CHAPTER 6

Final Years

Ever since 1905, when Einstein had shown that mass contains an equivalent amount of energy, scientists had wondered if there was any way of releasing the energy locked within the nucleus at the heart of an atom. The energy that might be obtained from one gram of uranium was 10,000 times the energy that could be released by burning a kilogram of coal. In 1905 the concept of **atomic power** was only a dream. By 1939, it was beginning to look as if it might be possible. Not only might the atom be used to provide power for the benefit of mankind, it could also be used to produce a bomb of unimaginable destructive power.

Many people were alarmed at this possibility. Germany had rebuilt its military in defiance of international treaties. In 1936 Germany had stationed troops in the Rhineland region. In 1938 Germany had annexed Austria; in 1939, Czechoslovakia. If Germany possessed the atomic bomb, how could the spread of Nazism be stopped? And much of our knowledge of the atomic nucleus had been gained in German laboratories.

Einstein became involved in the problem through his friendship with the Belgian royal family. The Belgian Congo was the main source of uranium ore. Einstein was asked by colleagues to write to Queen Elizabeth of Belgium, alerting her to the dangers that would arise should the Belgian ore be sold to the Germans. Eventually it was decided that he should write instead to the American president, Franklin Roosevelt (1882–1945), stressing that the construction of an atomic bomb might be possible. Presidents have much to do other than listen to the theories of physicists. They cannot read every letter they receive. So the power of Einstein's name was necessary to ensure that the message got through.

```
                                          Albert Einstein
                                          Old Grove Rd.
                                          Nassau Point
                                          Peconic, Long Island

                                          August 2nd, 1939

F.D. Roosevelt,
President of the United States,
White House
Washington, D.C.


Sir:

        Some recent work by E.Fermi and L. Szilard, which has been com-
municated to me in manuscript, leads me to expect that the element uran-
ium may be turned into a new and important source of energy in the im-
mediate future. Certain aspects of the situation which has arisen seem
to call for watchfulness and, if necessary, quick action on the part
of the Administration. I believe therefore that it is my duty to bring
to your attention the following facts and recommendations:

        In the course of the last four months it has been made probable -
through the work of Joliot in France as well as Fermi and Szilard in
America - that it may become possible to set up a nuclear chain reaction
in a large mass of uranium,by which vast amounts of power and large quant-
ities of new radium-like elements would be generated. Now it appears
almost certain that this could be achieved in the immediate future.

        This new phenomenon would also lead to the construction of bombs,
and it is conceivable - though much less certain - that extremely power-
ful bombs of a new type may thus be constructed. A single bomb of this
type, carried by boat and exploded in a port, might very well destroy
the whole port together with some of the surrounding territory. However,
such bombs might very well prove to be too heavy for transportation by
air.
```

Einstein's 1939 letter to Roosevelt, in which he warns that Germany might be working to-ward the development of nuclear weapons.

The United States has only very poor ores of uranium in moderate quantities. There is some good ore in Canada and the former Czechoslovakia, while the most important source of uranium is Belgian Congo.

In view of this situation you may think it desirable to have some permanent contact maintained between the Administration and the group of physicists working on chain reactions in America. One possible way of achieving this might be for you to entrust with this task a person who has your confidence and who could perhaps serve in an inofficial capacity. His task might comprise the following:

a) to approach Government Departments, keep them informed of the further development, and put forward recommendations for Government action, giving particular attention to the problem of securing a supply of uranium ore for the United States;

b) to speed up the experimental work,which is at present being carried on within the limits of the budgets of University laboratories, by providing funds, if such funds be required, through his contacts with private persons who are willing to make contributions for this cause, and perhaps also by obtaining the co-operation of industrial laboratories which have the necessary equipment.

I understand that Germany has actually stopped the sale of uranium from the Czechoslovakian mines which she has taken over. That she should have taken such early action might perhaps be understood on the ground that the son of the German Under-Secretary of State, von Weizsäcker, is attached to the Kaiser-Wilhelm-Institut in Berlin where some of the American work on uranium is now being repeated.

Yours very truly,

A. Einstein

(Albert Einstein)

A mushroom cloud rises more than 60,000 feet into the air over Nagasaki after an atomic bomb was dropped on the Japanese city. Einstein was horrified by the atomic bombings at the end of World War II. "If I had foreseen Hiroshima and Nagasaki, I would have torn up my formula in 1905," he told a friend in 1948.

The result of the letter was the formation of a committee, the Advisory Committee on Uranium. The dangers warranted action, and it was decided that Einstein should write a second letter. In the end the main impetus came from Britain, where scientists had succeeded in making the calculations that showed a bomb could definitely be made. In 1942 the work was transferred to the United States, and an all-out effort was mounted. No one could know until after the war that the German atomic bomb effort would never get beyond the drawing board.

As an American citizen, Einstein was willing to help the war effort in any way he could, but it was thought neither desirable nor necessary that he should know enough of the secrets of the bomb project to enable him to help effectively on that. He did, however, act as a consultant to the United States Navy, advising on various projects. He also helped to raise money for the war by selling two of his manuscripts, at a price of over $11 million.

Atomic Weapons

As the war in Europe neared its end, and the threat from Nazism receded, Einstein became increasingly aware of the dangers to the world from atomic weapons. If the United States could make an atomic bomb, it would be possible for other countries to make one too. It was difficult to get this across to the politicians. Bohr was treated as a possible spy for suggesting it. Again, Einstein's name was used to get a hearing for the scientists' views, but this time it was not enough. The U.S. government decided to use its atomic weapons, hoping they would hasten the end of the conflict.

In May 1945, Germany surrendered to the allied forces, but the war against Japan continued. In the United States, three atomic bombs were ready for use. On July 16, 1945, a huge mushroom cloud of smoke rising from the New Mexico desert signified that the first atomic bomb had been successfully tested. On August 6, 1945, an atomic bomb was dropped on the Japanese city of Hiroshima. Within seconds, much of the city was destroyed. More than 70,000 of Hiroshima's inhabitants were killed instantly, and another 70,000 were injured. Those who survived the blast, along with many unborn children, would suffer a lingering death from the effects of radiation.

Einstein's secretary heard the news on the radio. Over afternoon tea, she told the professor. The grief in his deep sigh could not be conveyed in words.

Another atomic bomb was dropped on the Japanese city of Nagasaki three days later. Within a week, the Japanese government surrendered, ending the Second World War.

For a video on Einstein and the atomic bomb, scan here:

Solving Problems

Einstein and others believed that with atomic bombs, future wars could destroy mankind. To prevent this from happening, Einstein believed it was important that there should be international control of atomic weapons.

He worked in whatever way he could toward a world government that would exercise such control. He presided over an emergency committee dedicated to making available to the public information about the implications of the bomb. As his last public act, he signed what has become known as the Einstein-Russell Declaration. This was drawn up with the great English philosopher Bertrand Russell (1872–1970), who was also concerned about the destruction caused by the atomic bomb. The aim of the declaration was to impress on governments and peoples the need to avoid war. This led to the establishment of the Pugwash Conferences, where scientists of all nations join together in the search for peace.

Einstein lived in this house at 112 Mercer Street in Princeton, New Jersey, from 1935 until his death in 1955.

Albert Einstein in retirement.

Shortly after the end of the war, Einstein retired from his professorship at the institute in Princeton. He still worked on, ignored for the most part by the world of physics. He knew that time was running out—that he might never achieve the final solution to the mystery of the universe. This was all the more reason why he should not waste a minute. But he had no false hopes. Later, in 1952, he wrote, "As to my work, it no longer amounts to much: I don't get many results any more and have to be content with playing the Elder Statesman and the Jewish Saint."

Einstein claimed he had no special talent, only an intense curiosity. He lived on work. Whatever he did, his scientific problems were always in his mind. His notebooks were always with him—when he went sailing on his yacht, or while he waited for a friend at the railway station. When playing the piano he would stop suddenly, saying "Now I have found it," and a scientific problem had been solved. He cut down unnecessary things to a minimum. It was not necessary to wear suits. Dressing up was to be avoided whenever possible.

The untidy traveler, with white windswept hair, was never Einstein acting a part for the newspapers. It was Einstein with his mind on what he considered to be more important things. He was genuinely modest. When dining at an Oxford college, the hall packed with students and dons, buzzing with excitement, he could honestly ask, "Is anything special happening tonight?"

Final Years

After his retirement Einstein would still work at the institute in the mornings, returning home at lunchtime to continue in his study there. The evenings he would spend reading to his severely crippled sister, Maja, until her death in 1951.

Einstein himself was not completely well. He had not been healthy since 1928 when, after an unexpected collapse, a heart condition was diagnosed. He underwent an operation in 1945, and another in 1948, but from 1950 the condition gradually worsened, and it prevented him from making any journeys abroad once he had settled in the United States.

In 1952 Chaim Weizmann, the first president of Israel, died. Who more suitable could be found to succeed him than the world's most famous living Jew? The prime minister of Israel and legislature of Israel contacted Einstein to ask whether he would accept the presidency. Einstein was honored, but he politely declined the offer. He could not associate himself with the pomp and ceremony—and tact—that the office would require. Besides, it would interfere with his work.

The end came in 1955, at the age of seventy-five. In severe pain, Einstein refused a further operation. It might have been possible to prolong his life, but Einstein believed that if it was time to die, so be it. He was moved to hospital where he recovered for a while and asked for his notebooks. But in his final days he would not find the **unified field theory** he had sought for so long. It would be left to succeeding generations to continue the search by different methods. On April 18, 1955, Einstein died in his sleep.

A million words were written about him when he died. Einstein would only have responded with his deep, hearty laugh. He wanted no public funeral, no acts of homage. His ashes, according to his wishes, were scattered in an undisclosed place.

TEXT-DEPENDENT QUESTIONS

1. On what Japanese cities were atomic weapons used in 1945?
2. What was the Einstein-Russell Declaration?

RESEARCH PROJECT

Using your school library or the internet, find out more about the Manhattan Project. Write a two-page report and share it with your class.

Chronology

1879
Albert Einstein is born on March 14 at Ulm, Germany.

1884
Begins attending the Catholic school in Munich, where he will study until 1889.

1889
Begins secondary education at the Luitpold Gymnasium in Munich.

1895
Fails the entrance examination to Zurich Polytechnic. Gives up his German nationality.

1896
Admitted to the Zurich Polytechnic, where he studies physics.

1900
Max Planck publishes his idea of "light quanta."

1901
Einstein adopts Swiss nationality.

1902
Begins work at the Patents Office in Berne.

1903
Marries Mileva Maric. Their first son, Hans Albert, is born.

1905
Publishes papers on Brownian motion, the photo-electric effect, and special relativity.

1907
Resolves the problem of the heat capacity of solids. First attempts at general theory of relativity.

1908
Appointed as *privatdozent* at Berne University.

1909
Appointed to professorship in Zurich. Leaves the Patents Office.

1910
Birth of Einstein's second son, Eduard.

1911
Einstein accepts a professorship in Prague.

1912
Appointed to professorship at Zurich Polytechnic.

1913
Joint publication with Marcel Grossmann on general relativity. Niels Bohr publishes his theory of the atom.

1914
Einstein is appointed to a professorship in Berlin. He separates from his wife, Mileva. Outbreak of the First World War.

1916
The final version of the general theory of relativity is published.

1917
"Einstein model" of the universe is published. Einstein discovers spontaneous emission of light from atoms. Suffers a breakdown.

1918
The First World War ends.

1919
Einstein is divorced from Mileva. He marries Elsa Lowenthal. Eddington's eclipse expedition confirms the bending of light by the sun.

1920
Einstein's mother dies. He resumes German citizenship.

1921
Makes his first visit to the U.S. and England.

1922
Awarded the Nobel Prize for Physics.

1923
Hitler's attempt to seize power in Munich fails.

1924
Einstein discovers the laws of probability applying to atoms.

1928

An unexpected collapse reveals heart trouble. He begins work on the "unified field theory."

1929

The critical work *100 Authors against Einstein* is published. Einstein's visit to the Belgian royal family marks the beginning of their friendship.

1933

Hitler and the Nazi Party come to power in Germany. Einstein leaves Europe for the United States, where he takes a position at the Institute for Advanced Study in Princeton, New Jersey.

1936

Einstein's second wife Elsa dies.

1938

Otto Hahn in Berlin splits the uranium nucleus.

1939

Einstein writes to President Roosevelt about the possibility of constructing an atomic bomb. The Second World War begins in September.

1941

Einstein adopts U.S. citizenship.

1945

Two atomic bombs are dropped on Japan; the Second World War ends.

1952

Einstein declines the presidency of Israel.

1955

Dies in Princeton on April 18, aged seventy-five.

Further Reading

Egdall, Ira Mark. *Einstein Relatively Simple: Our Universe Revealed in Everyday Language*. New York: World Scientific Publishing Co., 2014.

Einstein, Albert. *Relativity: The Special and General Theory*. Trans. Robert W. Lawson. New York: Digireads, 2017.

———. *The World as I See It*. New York: Snowball Publishing, 2014.

Isaacson, Walter. *Einstein: His Life and Universe*. New York: Simon & Schuster, 2007.

Kelly, Cynthia C., editor. *Manhattan Project: The Birth of the Atomic Bomb in the Words of its Creators, Eyewitnesses, and Historians*. New York: Black Dog & Leventhal Publishers, 2007.

Mermin, N. David. *It's About Time: Understanding Einstein's Relativity*. Princeton, N.J.: Princeton University Press, 2009.

Morus, Iwan Rhys. *The Oxford Illustrated History of Science*. New York: Oxford University Press, 2017.

Pohlen, Jerome. *Einstein and Relativity for Kids*. Chicago: Chicago Review Press, 2012.

Wootton, David. *The Invention of Science: A New History of the Scientific Revolution*. New York: Harper Perennial, 2016.

Internet Resources

http://www.albert-einstein.org

The website of the Albert Einstein Archives at the Hebrew University of Jerusalem includes a searchable database of Einstein's writings, a biography of the scientist, and many other resources.

https://history.aip.org/history/exhibits/einstein

The Center for the History of Physics, a project of the American Institute of Physics, manages this online exhibit exploring the life and scholarship of Albert Einstein.

https://www.sciencenewsforstudents.org

Science News for Students is an award-winning online publication dedicated to providing age-appropriate, topical science news to learners, parents and educators.

http://www.pbs.org/wgbh/nova

The website of *NOVA*, a science series that airs on PBS. The series produces in-depth science programming on a variety of topics, from the latest breakthroughs in technology to the deepest mysteries of the natural world.

https://www.physics.org/

This website from the Institute of Physics is intended to provide resources about physics to students of all ages.

Series Glossary of Key Terms

anomaly: something that differs from the expectations generated by an established scientific idea. Anomalous observations may inspire scientists to reconsider, modify, or come up with alternatives to an accepted theory or hypothesis.

evidence: test results and/or observations that may either help support or help refute a scientific idea. In general, raw data are considered evidence only once they have been interpreted in a way that reflects on the accuracy of a scientific idea.

experiment: a scientific test that involves manipulating some factor or factors in a system in order to see how those changes affect the outcome or behavior of the system.

hypothesis: a proposed explanation for a fairly narrow set of phenomena, usually based on prior experience, scientific background knowledge, preliminary observations, and logic.

natural world: all the components of the physical universe, as well as the natural forces at work on those things.

objective: to consider and represent facts without being influenced by biases, opinions, or emotions. Scientists strive to be objective, not subjective, in their reasoning about scientific issues.

observe: to note, record, or attend to a result, occurrence, or phenomenon.

science: knowledge of the natural world, as well as the process through which that knowledge is built through testing ideas with evidence gathered from the natural world.

subjective: referring to something that is influenced by biases, opinions, and/or emotions. Scientists strive to be objective, not subjective, in their reasoning about scientific issues.

test: an observation or experiment that could provide evidence regarding the accuracy of a scientific idea. Testing involves figuring out what one would expect to observe if an idea were correct and comparing that expectation to what one actually observes.

theory: a broad, natural explanation for a wide range of phenomena in science. Theories are concise, coherent, systematic, predictive, and broadly applicable, often integrating and generalizing many hypotheses. Theories accepted by the scientific community are generally strongly supported by many different lines of evidence. However, theories may be modified or overturned as new evidence is discovered.

Index

Newtonian theory, 54
Nobel Prize for Physics, 34, 36
notes, written by Einstein, 36
nuclear magnetic resonance, 70

O
Olympian Academy, 22

P
pacifist, 52, 66
Paris peace conference, 51
particles, 22, 23
Patents Office, 6, 17, 19, 22, 33
philosophy, 10
photo-electric effect, 69, 71
photographs (sun), 39–40
physics, study of, 7, 9, 10, 15, 69, 72
Planck, Max, 33, 34, 35, 66, 71
Pluto, 57
Poincaré, Henri, 26, 30
pollen grains, 24
polytechnic, 6, 15, 35
Polytechnic Institute (Zurich), 15, 16, 19, 35
postwar relations (Britian and Germany), 51
Principle of Special Relativity, 28, 43
privatdozent, 33
probability, 60, 72
Pugwash Conferences, 80

Q
quanta, 71
quantum, 60, 71
quantum physics, 72, 73

R
Rabi, Isidor Issac, 70
relative (motion), 27, 30
relativity, general theory of, 40 (QR code), 46, 54, 59, 61
Rhineland region (1936), 75
Roosevelt, Franklin, 75, 76–77
Royal Astronomical Society, 40
Rutherford, Ernest, 67, 71

S
scientific instruments, 7
scientific paper, 6, 17

Second Battle of Ypres (Belgium), 39
Second World War, 65, 80
Social Democrats, 34
solar system, 57
Solovine, Maurice, 22
space, 22
space and time, theory of, 24
space-travel timetable, 45
spacetime diagram, 18, 24 (QR code), 27–28, 44, 47, 57
Special theory of Relativity, 24, 29, 30, 35, 41, 46
static universe, 59
sub-atomic, 60, 69, 72
Swiss Civil Servant, 17, 19, 33

T
Talmey, Max, 10
teaching, as a profession, 22
telescope, 7
theoretical scientist, 49
time, 22
train (example of motion), 27, 28, 44

U
Ulm (Germany), 9, 10 (QR code), 12
unified field theory, 74, 84
uniform motion, 18, 27, 28, 43
universe, 6
uranium, 75

V
vapor, 7
violin, 10
Virgo supercluster, 57

W
war, opposition to, 39, 49, 51, 65, 79
Weizmann, Chaim, 83–84
Witowski, August, 33

Z
Zionism, 52, 53
Zurich University, 33

About the Author

Derrick Rain is a graduate of Boston College with a degree in physics. He currently teaches high school science in Worcester, Massachusetts. This is his first book.

Photo Credits